To:

_____

From:

_____

Date:

_____

Christian Art
GIFTS

© Christian Art Gifts, RSA
Christian Art Gifts Inc., IL, USA
Printed in Vietnam

"Be strong and courageous!
For the LORD your God is with you wherever you go."

JOSH. 1:9

He made us, and we are His. We are His people, the sheep of His pasture.

Ps. 100:3

Give your burdens to the LORD, and He will take care of you.

Ps. 55:22

Let God transform you into a new person by changing the way you think.

ROM. 12:2

"God blesses those who work for peace,
for they will be called the children of God."

Matt. 5:9

_____

"Anything is possible if a person believes."

I can do everything through Christ, who gives me strength.

PHIL. 4:13

_____

_____

_____

_____

_____

_____

_____

_____

_____

_____

_____

_____

_____

_____

_____

_____

_____

_____

_____

_____

_____

_____

_____

_____

"Blessed are those who trust in the Lᴏʀᴅ and have made
the Lᴏʀᴅ their hope and confidence."

Jᴇʀ. 17:7

The LORD leads with unfailing love and faithfulness
all who keep His covenant and obey His demands.

Ps. 25:10

"Come to Me, all of you who are weary and carry heavy burdens,
and I will give you rest."

MATT. 11:28

_____

_____
_____
_____
_____
_____
_____
_____
_____
_____
_____
_____
_____
_____
_____
_____
_____
_____
_____
_____
_____
_____
_____

"Do not be afraid or discouraged,
for the LORD will personally go ahead of you."

DEUT. 31:8

Those who live in the shelter of the Most High will find rest
in the shadow of the Almighty.

Ps. 91:1

"I will never fail you. I will never abandon you."

Heb. 13:5

Kind words are like honey – sweet to the soul and healthy for the body.

Prov. 16:24

The joy of the Lord is your strength!

Neh. 8:10

This is the day the LORD has made.
We will rejoice and be glad in it.

Ps. 118:24

Those who trust in the Lᴏʀᴅ will find new strength.
They will soar high on wings like eagles.

Iꜱᴀ. 40:31

"No eye has seen, no ear has heard, and no mind has imagined
what God has prepared for those who love Him."

1 Cor. 2:9

I will rejoice in the Lord! I will be joyful in the God of my salvation!

Nothing in all creation will ever be able to separate us from the love of God.

My health may fail, and my spirit may grow weak, but God remains
the strength of my heart; He is mine forever.

Ps. 73:26

_____

_____

_____

_____

_____

_____

_____

_____

_____

_____

_____

_____

_____

_____

_____

_____

_____

_____

_____

_____

_____

_____

_____

_____

See how very much our Father loves us, for He calls us
His children, and that is what we are!

1 JOHN 3:1

"Blessed are all who hear the word of God
and put it into practice."

Luke 11:28

The LORD is my light and my salvation –
so why should I be afraid?

Ps. 27:1

The Lord is my strength and my song; He has given me victory.
This is my God, and I will praise Him.

Exod. 15:2

May the Lord of peace Himself give you His peace
at all times and in every situation.

2 Thess. 3:16

Let the peace that comes from Christ rule in your hearts.
For as members of one body you are called to live in peace.

Col. 3:15

LORD my God, I cried to You for help, and You restored my health.

"Those who exalt themselves will be humbled,
and those who humble themselves will be exalted."

Matt. 23:12

_____

"Do not be afraid, for I have ransomed you. I have called you by name;
you are Mine. When you go through deep waters, I will be with you."

Isa. 43:1-2

"Be still, and know that I am God!"

Ps. 46:10

"I know the plans I have for you," says the LORD. "They are plans for good and not for disaster, to give you a future and a hope."

JER. 29:11

"Be strong and courageous!
For the LORD your God is with you wherever you go."

JOSH. 1:9

He made us, and we are His. We are His people, the sheep of His pasture.

Ps. 100:3

Give your burdens to the Lord, and He will take care of you.

Ps. 55:22

Let God transform you into a new person by changing the way you think.

"God blesses those who work for peace,
for they will be called the children of God."

Matt. 5:9

"Anything is possible if a person believes."

MARK 9:23

I can do everything through Christ, who gives me strength.

PHIL. 4:13

"Blessed are those who trust in the Lord and have made
the Lord their hope and confidence."

Jer. 17:7

The Lord leads with unfailing love and faithfulness
all who keep His covenant and obey His demands.

Ps. 25:10

"Come to Me, all of you who are weary and carry heavy burdens, and I will give you rest."

MATT. 11:28

"Do not be afraid or discouraged,
for the LORD will personally go ahead of you."

DEUT. 31:8

Those who live in the shelter of the Most High will find rest
in the shadow of the Almighty.

Ps. 91:1

"I will never fail you. I will never abandon you."

Heb. 13:5

Kind words are like honey – sweet to the soul and healthy for the body.

PROV. 16:24

The joy of the Lord is your strength!

Neh. 8:10

This is the day the LORD has made.
We will rejoice and be glad in it.

Ps. 118:24

Those who trust in the LORD will find new strength.
They will soar high on wings like eagles.

ISA. 40:31

_____

_____

_____

_____

_____

_____

_____

_____

_____

_____

_____

_____

_____

_____

_____

_____

_____

_____

_____

_____

_____

_____

"No eye has seen, no ear has heard, and no mind has imagined
what God has prepared for those who love Him."

1 Cor. 2:9

I will rejoice in the LORD! I will be joyful in the God of my salvation!

Nothing in all creation will ever be able to separate us from the love of God.

My health may fail, and my spirit may grow weak, but God remains
the strength of my heart; He is mine forever.

Ps. 73:26

See how very much our Father loves us, for He calls us
His children, and that is what we are!

1 John 3:1

"Blessed are all who hear the word of God
and put it into practice."

The LORD is my light and my salvation –
so why should I be afraid?

Ps. 27:1

The LORD is my strength and my song; He has given me victory.
This is my God, and I will praise Him.

EXOD. 15:2

May the Lord of peace Himself give you His peace
at all times and in every situation.

2 Thess. 3:16

Let the peace that comes from Christ rule in your hearts.
For as members of one body you are called to live in peace.

COL. 3:15

LORD my God, I cried to You for help, and You restored my health.

Ps. 30:2

"Those who exalt themselves will be humbled,
and those who humble themselves will be exalted."

Matt. 23:12

"Do not be afraid, for I have ransomed you. I have called you by name; you are Mine. When you go through deep waters, I will be with you."

Isa. 43:1-2

"Be still, and know that I am God!"

Ps. 46:10

_____

"I know the plans I have for you," says the Lord. "They are plans for good and not for disaster, to give you a future and a hope."

JER. 29:11

He made us, and we are His. We are His people, the sheep of His pasture.

Ps. 100:3

Give your burdens to the LORD, and He will take care of you.

Ps. 55:22

Let God transform you into a new person by changing the way you think.

"God blesses those who work for peace,
for they will be called the children of God."

MATT. 5:9

_____

"Anything is possible if a person believes."

I can do everything through Christ, who gives me strength.

PHIL. 4:13

"Blessed are those who trust in the Lord and have made
the Lord their hope and confidence."

Jer. 17:7

The Lord leads with unfailing love and faithfulness
all who keep His covenant and obey His demands.

Ps. 25:10

_____

"Come to Me, all of you who are weary and carry heavy burdens,
and I will give you rest."

MATT. 11:28

"Do not be afraid or discouraged,
for the Lord will personally go ahead of you."

Deut. 31:8

Those who live in the shelter of the Most High will find rest
in the shadow of the Almighty.

Ps. 91:1

Kind words are like honey – sweet to the soul and healthy for the body.

The joy of the LORD is your strength!

NEH. 8:10

This is the day the LORD has made.
We will rejoice and be glad in it.

Ps. 118:24

Those who trust in the Lord will find new strength.
They will soar high on wings like eagles.

Isa. 40:31

"No eye has seen, no ear has heard, and no mind has imagined
what God has prepared for those who love Him."

1 Cor. 2:9

I will rejoice in the Lord! I will be joyful in the God of my salvation!

Nothing in all creation will ever be able to separate us from the love of God.

My health may fail, and my spirit may grow weak, but God remains
the strength of my heart; He is mine forever.

See how very much our Father loves us, for He calls us
His children, and that is what we are!

1 John 3:1

"Blessed are all who hear the word of God
and put it into practice."

LUKE 11:28

The Lord is my light and my salvation –
so why should I be afraid?

Ps. 27:1

The Lord is my strength and my song; He has given me victory.
This is my God, and I will praise Him.

Exod. 15:2

May the Lord of peace Himself give you His peace
at all times and in every situation.

2 THESS. 3:16

Let the peace that comes from Christ rule in your hearts.
For as members of one body you are called to live in peace.

Col. 3:15

Lord my God, I cried to You for help, and You restored my health.

Ps. 30:2

"Those who exalt themselves will be humbled,
and those who humble themselves will be exalted."

MATT. 23:12

"Do not be afraid, for I have ransomed you. I have called you by name; you are Mine. When you go through deep waters, I will be with you."

Isa. 43:1-2

"Be still, and know that I am God!"

Ps. 46:10

"I know the plans I have for you," says the LORD. "They are plans for good and not for disaster, to give you a future and a hope."

JER. 29:11

He made us, and we are His. We are His people, the sheep of His pasture.

Ps. 100:3

Give your burdens to the LORD, and He will take care of you.

Ps. 55:22

Let God transform you into a new person by changing the way you think.

Rom. 12:2

"God blesses those who work for peace,
for they will be called the children of God."

MATT. 5:9

_____

"Anything is possible if a person believes."

I can do everything through Christ, who gives me strength.

Phil. 4:13

"Blessed are those who trust in the LORD and have made
the LORD their hope and confidence."

JER. 17:7

The Lord leads with unfailing love and faithfulness
all who keep His covenant and obey His demands.

Ps. 25:10

_____

"Come to Me, all of you who are weary and carry heavy burdens,
and I will give you rest."

MATT. 11:28

"Do not be afraid or discouraged,
for the LORD will personally go ahead of you."

DEUT. 31:8

Those who live in the shelter of the Most High will find rest
in the shadow of the Almighty.

Ps. 91:1

Kind words are like honey – sweet to the soul and healthy for the body.

The joy of the LORD is your strength!

NEH. 8:10

This is the day the LORD has made.
We will rejoice and be glad in it.

Ps. 118:24

Those who trust in the LORD will find new strength.
They will soar high on wings like eagles.

ISA. 40:31

"No eye has seen, no ear has heard, and no mind has imagined
what God has prepared for those who love Him."

1 Cor. 2:9

I will rejoice in the LORD! I will be joyful in the God of my salvation!

HAB. 3:18

Nothing in all creation will ever be able to separate us from the love of God.

My health may fail, and my spirit may grow weak, but God remains
the strength of my heart; He is mine forever.

Ps. 73:26

See how very much our Father loves us, for He calls us
His children, and that is what we are!

1 JOHN 3:1

_____

The LORD is my light and my salvation –
so why should I be afraid?

Ps. 27:1

The Lord is my strength and my song; He has given me victory.
This is my God, and I will praise Him.

Exod. 15:2

May the Lord of peace Himself give you His peace
at all times and in every situation.

2 Thess. 3:16

Let the peace that comes from Christ rule in your hearts.
For as members of one body you are called to live in peace.

Col. 3:15

Lᴏʀᴅ my God, I cried to You for help, and You restored my health.

Ps. 30:2

"Those who exalt themselves will be humbled,
and those who humble themselves will be exalted."

MATT. 23:12

"Do not be afraid, for I have ransomed you. I have called you by name;
you are Mine. When you go through deep waters, I will be with you."

Isa. 43:1-2

"Be still, and know that I am God!"

Ps. 46:10

"I know the plans I have for you," says the LORD. "They are plans for good and not for disaster, to give you a future and a hope."

JER. 29:11

"Be strong and courageous!
For the Lord your God is with you wherever you go."

Josh. 1:9

He made us, and we are His. We are His people, the sheep of His pasture.

Give your burdens to the LORD, and He will take care of you.

Ps. 55:22

Let God transform you into a new person by changing the way you think.

Rom. 12:2

"God blesses those who work for peace,
for they will be called the children of God."

MATT. 5:9

_____

"Anything is possible if a person believes."

MARK 9:23

I can do everything through Christ, who gives me strength.

"Blessed are those who trust in the LORD and have made the LORD their hope and confidence."

JER. 17:7

The LORD leads with unfailing love and faithfulness
all who keep His covenant and obey His demands.

"Come to Me, all of you who are weary and carry heavy burdens,
and I will give you rest."

Matt. 11:28

Those who live in the shelter of the Most High will find rest
in the shadow of the Almighty.

Ps. 91:1

"I will never fail you. I will never abandon you."

HEB. 13:5

Kind words are like honey – sweet to the soul and healthy for the body.

The joy of the Lord is your strength!

Neh. 8:10

This is the day the LORD has made.
We will rejoice and be glad in it.

Ps. 118:24

Those who trust in the LORD will find new strength.
They will soar high on wings like eagles.

ISA. 40:31

_____

"No eye has seen, no ear has heard, and no mind has imagined
what God has prepared for those who love Him."

1 Cor. 2:9

I will rejoice in the LORD! I will be joyful in the God of my salvation!

Nothing in all creation will ever be able to separate us from the love of God.

Rom. 8:39

My health may fail, and my spirit may grow weak, but God remains
the strength of my heart; He is mine forever.

Ps. 73:26

See how very much our Father loves us, for He calls us
His children, and that is what we are!

1 John 3:1

"Blessed are all who hear the word of God
and put it into practice."

Luke 11:28

The LORD is my light and my salvation –
so why should I be afraid?

Ps. 27:1

The LORD is my strength and my song; He has given me victory.
This is my God, and I will praise Him.

EXOD. 15:2

_____

_____

_____

_____

_____

_____

_____

_____

_____

_____

_____

_____

_____

_____

_____

_____

_____

_____

_____

_____

_____

_____

_____

_____

May the Lord of peace Himself give you His peace
at all times and in every situation.

2 THESS. 3:16

Let the peace that comes from Christ rule in your hearts.
For as members of one body you are called to live in peace.

Col. 3:15

Lord my God, I cried to You for help, and You restored my health.

Ps. 30:2

"Those who exalt themselves will be humbled,
and those who humble themselves will be exalted."

MATT. 23:12

_____

_____

_____

_____

_____

_____

_____

_____

_____

_____

_____

_____

_____

_____

_____

_____

_____

_____

_____

_____

_____

_____

_____

_____

_____

"Do not be afraid, for I have ransomed you. I have called you by name; you are Mine. When you go through deep waters, I will be with you."

Isa. 43:1-2

"Be still, and know that I am God!"

Ps. 46:10

"I know the plans I have for you," says the LORD. "They are plans for good and not for disaster, to give you a future and a hope."

JER. 29:11

He made us, and we are His. We are His people, the sheep of His pasture.

Ps. 100:3

Give your burdens to the LORD, and He will take care of you.

Ps. 55:22

Let God transform you into a new person by changing the way you think.

Rom. 12:2

"God blesses those who work for peace,
for they will be called the children of God."

MATT. 5:9

"Anything is possible if a person believes."

MARK 9:23

I can do everything through Christ, who gives me strength.

"Blessed are those who trust in the LORD and have made
the LORD their hope and confidence."

The Lord leads with unfailing love and faithfulness
all who keep His covenant and obey His demands.

Ps. 25:10

"Come to Me, all of you who are weary and carry heavy burdens, and I will give you rest."

MATT. 11:28

"Do not be afraid or discouraged,
for the LORD will personally go ahead of you."

Deut. 31:8

Those who live in the shelter of the Most High will find rest
in the shadow of the Almighty.

Ps. 91:1

"I will never fail you. I will never abandon you."

Heb. 13:5

Kind words are like honey – sweet to the soul and healthy for the body.

PROV. 16:24

The joy of the LORD is your strength!

NEH. 8:10

This is the day the LORD has made.
We will rejoice and be glad in it.

Ps. 118:24

Those who trust in the LORD will find new strength.
They will soar high on wings like eagles.

Isa. 40:31

"No eye has seen, no ear has heard, and no mind has imagined
what God has prepared for those who love Him."

1 COR. 2:9

I will rejoice in the LORD! I will be joyful in the God of my salvation!

Nothing in all creation will ever be able to separate us from the love of God.

ROM. 8:39

My health may fail, and my spirit may grow weak, but God remains
the strength of my heart; He is mine forever.

Ps. 73:26

See how very much our Father loves us, for He calls us
His children, and that is what we are!

1 John 3:1

"Blessed are all who hear the word of God
and put it into practice."

LUKE 11:28

The LORD is my light and my salvation –
so why should I be afraid?

Ps. 27:1

The Lord is my strength and my song; He has given me victory.
This is my God, and I will praise Him.

Exod. 15:2

May the Lord of peace Himself give you His peace
at all times and in every situation.

2 Thess. 3:16

Let the peace that comes from Christ rule in your hearts.
For as members of one body you are called to live in peace.

COL. 3:15

Lord my God, I cried to You for help, and You restored my health.

Ps. 30:2

_____

_____

_____

_____

_____

_____

_____

_____

_____

_____

_____

_____

_____

_____

_____

_____

_____

_____

_____

_____

_____

_____

_____

_____

"Those who exalt themselves will be humbled,
and those who humble themselves will be exalted."

MATT. 23:12

_____

"Do not be afraid, for I have ransomed you. I have called you by name;
you are Mine. When you go through deep waters, I will be with you."

Isa. 43:1-2

"Be still, and know that I am God!"

Ps. 46:10

"I know the plans I have for you," says the LORD. "They are plans for good
and not for disaster, to give you a future and a hope."

JER. 29:11

"Be strong and courageous!
For the Lord your God is with you wherever you go."

He made us, and we are His. We are His people, the sheep of His pasture.

Ps. 100:3

Give your burdens to the LORD, and He will take care of you.

Ps. 55:22

Let God transform you into a new person by changing the way you think.

"God blesses those who work for peace,
for they will be called the children of God."

MATT. 5:9

_____

"Anything is possible if a person believes."

MARK 9:23

I can do everything through Christ, who gives me strength.

PHIL. 4:13

"Blessed are those who trust in the LORD and have made
the LORD their hope and confidence."

JER. 17:7

The LORD leads with unfailing love and faithfulness
all who keep His covenant and obey His demands.

"Come to Me, all of you who are weary and carry heavy burdens,
and I will give you rest."

"Do not be afraid or discouraged,
for the LORD will personally go ahead of you."

DEUT. 31:8

Those who live in the shelter of the Most High will find rest
in the shadow of the Almighty.

Ps. 91:1

"I will never fail you. I will never abandon you."

Kind words are like honey – sweet to the soul and healthy for the body.

Prov. 16:24

The joy of the Lord is your strength!

Neh. 8:10

This is the day the LORD has made.
We will rejoice and be glad in it.

Ps. 118:24

Those who trust in the Lᴏʀᴅ will find new strength.
They will soar high on wings like eagles.

Isᴀ. 40:31

"No eye has seen, no ear has heard, and no mind has imagined
what God has prepared for those who love Him."

1 Cor. 2:9

I will rejoice in the Lord! I will be joyful in the God of my salvation!

Hab. 3:18

Nothing in all creation will ever be able to separate us from the love of God.

My health may fail, and my spirit may grow weak, but God remains
the strength of my heart; He is mine forever.

Ps. 73:26

See how very much our Father loves us, for He calls us
His children, and that is what we are!

1 John 3:1

"Blessed are all who hear the word of God
and put it into practice."

LUKE 11:28

The Lord is my light and my salvation –
so why should I be afraid?

Ps. 27:1

The Lord is my strength and my song; He has given me victory.
This is my God, and I will praise Him.

Exod. 15:2

May the Lord of peace Himself give you His peace
at all times and in every situation.

2 Thess. 3:16

Let the peace that comes from Christ rule in your hearts.
For as members of one body you are called to live in peace.

Lord my God, I cried to You for help, and You restored my health.

Ps. 30:2

"Those who exalt themselves will be humbled,
and those who humble themselves will be exalted."

MATT. 23:12

"Do not be afraid, for I have ransomed you. I have called you by name; you are Mine. When you go through deep waters, I will be with you."

Isa. 43:1-2

"Be still, and know that I am God!"

Ps. 46:10

_____

_____

_____

_____

_____

_____

_____

_____

_____

_____

_____

_____

_____

_____

_____

_____

_____

_____

_____

_____

_____

_____

_____

"I know the plans I have for you," says the LORD. "They are plans for good and not for disaster, to give you a future and a hope."

JER. 29:11

He made us, and we are His. We are His people, the sheep of His pasture.

Ps. 100:3

Give your burdens to the LORD, and He will take care of you.

Ps. 55:22

Let God transform you into a new person by changing the way you think.

ROM. 12:2

"God blesses those who work for peace,
for they will be called the children of God."

MATT. 5:9

"Anything is possible if a person believes."

I can do everything through Christ, who gives me strength.

"Blessed are those who trust in the LORD and have made
the LORD their hope and confidence."

JER. 17:7

The Lord leads with unfailing love and faithfulness
all who keep His covenant and obey His demands.

Ps. 25:10

_____

"Come to Me, all of you who are weary and carry heavy burdens,
and I will give you rest."

MATT. 11:28

Those who live in the shelter of the Most High will find rest
in the shadow of the Almighty.

Ps. 91:1

"I will never fail you. I will never abandon you."

HEB. 13:5

Kind words are like honey – sweet to the soul and healthy for the body.

PROV. 16:24

The joy of the LORD is your strength!

NEH. 8:10

This is the day the Lord has made.
We will rejoice and be glad in it.

Ps. 118:24

Those who trust in the Lord will find new strength.
They will soar high on wings like eagles.

Isa. 40:31

"No eye has seen, no ear has heard, and no mind has imagined what God has prepared for those who love Him."

1 Cor. 2:9

I will rejoice in the LORD! I will be joyful in the God of my salvation!

HAB. 3:18

Nothing in all creation will ever be able to separate us from the love of God.

ROM. 8:39

My health may fail, and my spirit may grow weak, but God remains
the strength of my heart; He is mine forever.

Ps. 73:26

See how very much our Father loves us, for He calls us
His children, and that is what we are!

1 John 3:1

The Lord is my light and my salvation –
so why should I be afraid?

Ps. 27:1

The LORD is my strength and my song; He has given me victory.
This is my God, and I will praise Him.

EXOD. 15:2

_____

_____

_____

_____

_____

_____

_____

_____

_____

_____

_____

_____

_____

_____

_____

_____

_____

_____

_____

_____

_____

May the Lord of peace Himself give you His peace
at all times and in every situation.

2 THESS. 3:16

Let the peace that comes from Christ rule in your hearts.
For as members of one body you are called to live in peace.

Col. 3:15

LORD my God, I cried to You for help, and You restored my health.

Ps. 30:2

"Those who exalt themselves will be humbled,
and those who humble themselves will be exalted."

"Do not be afraid, for I have ransomed you. I have called you by name; you are Mine. When you go through deep waters, I will be with you."

Isa. 43:1-2

"Be still, and know that I am God!"

Ps. 46:10

"I know the plans I have for you," says the LORD. "They are plans for good and not for disaster, to give you a future and a hope."

JER. 29:11

"Be strong and courageous!
For the LORD your God is with you wherever you go."

JOSH. 1:9

He made us, and we are His. We are His people, the sheep of His pasture.

Ps. 100:3

Give your burdens to the LORD, and He will take care of you.

Ps. 55:22

Let God transform you into a new person by changing the way you think.

Rom. 12:2

"God blesses those who work for peace,
for they will be called the children of God."

MATT. 5:9

_____

"Anything is possible if a person believes."

I can do everything through Christ, who gives me strength.

PHIL. 4:13

"Blessed are those who trust in the LORD and have made
the LORD their hope and confidence."

JER. 17:7

The Lord leads with unfailing love and faithfulness
all who keep His covenant and obey His demands.

Ps. 25:10

_____

_____

_____

_____

_____

_____

_____

_____

_____

_____

_____

_____

_____

_____

_____

_____

_____

_____

_____

"Come to Me, all of you who are weary and carry heavy burdens,
and I will give you rest."

Matt. 11:28

Those who live in the shelter of the Most High will find rest
in the shadow of the Almighty.

Ps. 91:1

"I will never fail you. I will never abandon you."

Heb. 13:5

Kind words are like honey – sweet to the soul and healthy for the body.

PROV. 16:24

The joy of the Lord is your strength!

Neh. 8:10

_____

_____

_____

_____

_____

_____

_____

_____

_____

_____

_____

_____

_____

_____

_____

_____

_____

_____

_____

_____

_____

_____

This is the day the LORD has made.
We will rejoice and be glad in it.

Ps. 118:24

Those who trust in the LORD will find new strength.
They will soar high on wings like eagles.

ISA. 40:31

_____

"No eye has seen, no ear has heard, and no mind has imagined
what God has prepared for those who love Him."

1 Cor. 2:9

I will rejoice in the LORD! I will be joyful in the God of my salvation!

HAB. 3:18

Nothing in all creation will ever be able to separate us from the love of God.

My health may fail, and my spirit may grow weak, but God remains
the strength of my heart; He is mine forever.

Ps. 73:26

See how very much our Father loves us, for He calls us
His children, and that is what we are!

1 John 3:1

"Blessed are all who hear the word of God
and put it into practice."

LUKE 11:28

The Lord is my light and my salvation –
so why should I be afraid?

Ps. 27:1

The Lord is my strength and my song; He has given me victory.
This is my God, and I will praise Him.

Exod. 15:2

May the Lord of peace Himself give you His peace
at all times and in every situation.

2 THESS. 3:16

Let the peace that comes from Christ rule in your hearts.
For as members of one body you are called to live in peace.

CoL. 3:15

Lord my God, I cried to You for help, and You restored my health.

Ps. 30:2

"Those who exalt themselves will be humbled,
and those who humble themselves will be exalted."

MATT. 23:12

_____

"Do not be afraid, for I have ransomed you. I have called you by name;
you are Mine. When you go through deep waters, I will be with you."

Isa. 43:1-2

"Be still, and know that I am God!"

Ps. 46:10

"I know the plans I have for you," says the LORD. "They are plans for good and not for disaster, to give you a future and a hope."

JER. 29:11

"Be strong and courageous!
For the LORD your God is with you wherever you go."

JOSH. 1:9

He made us, and we are His. We are His people, the sheep of His pasture.

Ps. 100:3

Give your burdens to the LORD, and He will take care of you.

Ps. 55:22

Let God transform you into a new person by changing the way you think.

"God blesses those who work for peace,
for they will be called the children of God."

Matt. 5:9

_____

"Anything is possible if a person believes."

MARK 9:23

I can do everything through Christ, who gives me strength.

PHIL. 4:13

"Blessed are those who trust in the LORD and have made
the LORD their hope and confidence."

JER. 17:7

The Lord leads with unfailing love and faithfulness
all who keep His covenant and obey His demands.

Ps. 25:10

"Come to Me, all of you who are weary and carry heavy burdens,
and I will give you rest."

Matt. 11:28

"Do not be afraid or discouraged,
for the Lord will personally go ahead of you."

Deut. 31:8

_____

Those who live in the shelter of the Most High will find rest
in the shadow of the Almighty.

Ps. 91:1

"I will never fail you. I will never abandon you."

Heb. 13:5

Kind words are like honey – sweet to the soul and healthy for the body.

The joy of the Lord is your strength!

Neh. 8:10

This is the day the Lord has made.
We will rejoice and be glad in it.

Ps. 118:24

Those who trust in the LORD will find new strength.
They will soar high on wings like eagles.

Isa. 40:31

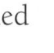

"No eye has seen, no ear has heard, and no mind has imagined
what God has prepared for those who love Him."

1 Cor. 2:9

I will rejoice in the LORD! I will be joyful in the God of my salvation!

HAB. 3:18

Nothing in all creation will ever be able to separate us from the love of God.

My health may fail, and my spirit may grow weak, but God remains
the strength of my heart; He is mine forever.

Ps. 73:26

See how very much our Father loves us, for He calls us
His children, and that is what we are!

1 John 3:1

"Blessed are all who hear the word of God
and put it into practice."

The Lord is my light and my salvation –
so why should I be afraid?

Ps. 27:1

The Lord is my strength and my song; He has given me victory.
This is my God, and I will praise Him.

Exod. 15:2

May the Lord of peace Himself give you His peace
at all times and in every situation.

Let the peace that comes from Christ rule in your hearts.
For as members of one body you are called to live in peace.

Col. 3:15

Lord my God, I cried to You for help, and You restored my health.

Ps. 30:2

"Those who exalt themselves will be humbled,
and those who humble themselves will be exalted."

MATT. 23:12

_____

"Do not be afraid, for I have ransomed you. I have called you by name;
you are Mine. When you go through deep waters, I will be with you."

Isa. 43:1-2

"Be still, and know that I am God!"

Ps. 46:10

"I know the plans I have for you," says the LORD. "They are plans for good and not for disaster, to give you a future and a hope."

JER. 29:11

"Be strong and courageous!
For the LORD your God is with you wherever you go."

JOSH. 1:9

He made us, and we are His. We are His people, the sheep of His pasture.

Ps. 100:3

Give your burdens to the LORD, and He will take care of you.

Ps. 55:22

Let God transform you into a new person by changing the way you think.

"God blesses those who work for peace,
for they will be called the children of God."

"Anything is possible if a person believes."

MARK 9:23

I can do everything through Christ, who gives me strength.

PHIL. 4:13

_____

_____

_____

_____

_____

_____

_____

_____

_____

_____

_____

_____

_____

_____

_____

_____

_____

_____

_____

_____

_____

"Blessed are those who trust in the Lord and have made
the Lord their hope and confidence."

Jer. 17:7

The Lord leads with unfailing love and faithfulness
all who keep His covenant and obey His demands.

Ps. 25:10

"Come to Me, all of you who are weary and carry heavy burdens,
and I will give you rest."

Matt. 11:28

"Do not be afraid or discouraged,
for the LORD will personally go ahead of you."

DEUT. 31:8

Those who live in the shelter of the Most High will find rest
in the shadow of the Almighty.

Ps. 91:1

"I will never fail you. I will never abandon you."

Heb. 13:5

Kind words are like honey – sweet to the soul and healthy for the body.